BOLD PARENTING

RAISING KIDS TO BE MORE THAN JUST RULE-KEEPERS

BY
DR. LARS ROOD

(†) simply for parents

YouthMinistry.com/TOGETHER

Bold Parenting
Raising Kids to Be More Than Just Rule-Keepers

Copyright © 2013 Dr. Lars Rood

group.com
simplyyouthministry.com

Credits
Author: Dr. Lars Rood
Executive Developer: Jason Ostrander
Chief Creative Officer: Joani Schultz
Editor: Rob Cunningham
Art Director: Veronica Preston
Production Manager: DeAnne Lear

ISBN 978-0-7644-9008-8

10 9 8 7 6 5 4 3   20 19 18 17 16 15

Printed in the United States of America.

Thanks to my mom and dad. You put up with a lot and are still around to see me get it about half right half of the time. That's got to feel good.

TABLE OF CONTENTS

BOLD PARENTING

INTRODUCTION

I'm not a perfect parent. Far from it, actually.

I struggle to know how to best teach my kids about Jesus. I worry that the faith I model (yes, even as a pastor) is a faith that's weak, spineless, without conviction, and lacking any sort of life-altering change that will help my children be different. And if I'm totally honest, I sometimes think more about my kids' future jobs than I do about their walk with Jesus when they will be 23.

The goal of this book isn't to shame anyone into changing the way they parent or think about faith. But the reality is that many of us need some major changes in how we pass on our faith to our kids. That's why it's easiest upfront to admit that much of what I discuss in this book points back at myself.

I hope that collectively we all can be OK with taking a good, long look at our own faith journey and can be honest and transparent about the places where we struggle and need to grow. I'll share a lot of stories about my failures, and I hope my honesty and transparency will help you.

This book has been a long time coming. About five years ago I participated in a cohort group put together by Dietrich Kirk and the Center for Youth Ministry Training. Not sure why I got invited to an event that had so many Ph.D. candidates and really strong writers and thinkers, but there I was at a table discussing the National Study on Youth and Religion. At one point during the conversation, I simply stated that I felt like oftentimes we parents only cared about the morality of our kids, and if we knew that the church would just help our kids to be "sober" and "virgins" when they graduated from high school, we would feel like we had accomplished the goal. That thought led into numerous conversations over the years about ministry, the church, the family, and ultimately what we are hoping to accomplish in the church.

So what's the goal here? It's for us to connect for the first time (or reconnect) to a faith that is vibrant and exciting. It's a faith that says, "Jesus, you are my all, and in following you I sacrifice my own will." It's a life that looks very different from trying to keep up with the neighbors and their new cars, vacations, jobs, and fancy lives. Not that those things are necessarily bad, but when we focus on them instead of what Jesus would have us do, we lose—as do our kids.

I remember a conversation I had once with a 30-year-old dad. He was expressing a strong desire to go on the mission field and, in his words, "do some actual good" with his life and faith. As he talked his face lit up about what it would look like to toss everything and raise his kids following Jesus, living overseas, and having a significant impact for the kingdom. But then his face fell and he said, "But I made my own bed and now have to sleep in it"—alluding to the fact that he had student loan debt, a mortgage, car payments, and a life that really didn't allow room for Jesus to initiate any change.

But I believe that we as parents must be willing to give Jesus room to change us, to challenge us. I read the book *Radical* by David Platt a few years back, and it really pushed my faith. That book encouraged me to break free of all that was holding back my faith and to celebrate making big and small steps to live a more radical Christian life. My hope, as you read my book, is that you would begin to think about how you can make "little" steps to your faith journey. Those little steps can add up over time to absolutely transform your faith and what you are passing on to your kids.

And I believe that when you become a "bold parent," you will see Jesus do amazing things. Your kids will be confident, they will know they are loved, they will see purpose and direction to their lives, and ultimately they will know those things come from Jesus and not from this world.

The key word you will hear over and over in this book is *bold*. When I use that word, I am particularly pointing to actions that follow the path of Jesus. To be bold means we do what Jesus did—and would do. He was countercultural, and he cared about things beyond himself. He was in tune with God, and the work of the Father was more important to him than the world. Jesus recognized that his role was to do "God's will" and not his own.

When I talk about "bold parenting," I specifically want to encourage you to live a life and parent in ways that Jesus might have if he'd been a parent. We want to help our kids follow Jesus, and that means they will care about the things he cares about—their lives will reflect his passions and priorities. It means we will make major steps to ensure that our families live and care about the things Jesus cares about. We will free ourselves from the pitfalls and struggles of the world and follow Jesus. In a practical way, this means having our kids serve the homeless and the poor at a soup kitchen might be more important than playing youth soccer. It means that when they are applying for college, we are praying about God putting them where he wants to grow them, more than putting them in a place where we think they will be successful and get a good job.

So here we go on the journey together. We will begin by talking about the problems. This first section might feel depressing because, ultimately, we are a large part of the problem. The weak faith and low standards that we have set for ourselves are being transferred to our kids. But it's also more than us. The church (which is us, too) has picked up on this and has lowered its standards. This must change.

The second section of this book focuses on what our kids really need. We'll take big stabs at why kids need to know who Jesus really is and what he truly wants for them. We'll look at expectations and dreams, plus a chapter centered on our own faith. You'll need to be prepared because some of this might be hard to hear. We must sit and think about the difference between what our kids really need and what we feel like we need to give them.

The last part of this book examines tools to move forward. This section should be the most encouraging because not all the steps we need to make are hard. We'll look at how to best pass on faith to our kids and what we can do to ensure that they have the best opportunities to be loved, cared for, and challenged in our families and churches.

Have I forgotten anything? Probably, but that's the great thing about Jesus. I'm going to try to set the stage for us to grow together—and at the same time I'm praying that Jesus fills in the gaps of anything that I forget. Each chapter ends with some study questions that can help you think about what changes you need to make—or things you need to keep doing. These questions are done best in community. So read this with a spouse, friend, or small group, and take time to collectively figure it out.

A special note for my friends in children's and youth ministry: I have written this book for parents, but even if you are not yet a parent, you can benefit from the things I share. When I write about "your children" or "our kids," simply transfer those principles to your interactions with the young people in your ministry. These chapters will help you work with children and youth, and these ideas will equip you to talk more effectively with parents. Plus, this book can also help you build a solid foundation as a future parent.

PART 1:
UNDERSTANDING THE PROBLEM

I think the problem is actually simple to see: The number of people following Jesus appears to be on a decline in the United States. And I suspect that most of us are not happy about that reality. We wish we lived in a society that cared about our families' spiritual lives as much as it cares about our financial lives. We want society to affirm that having faith matters. We want the faith that we are passing down to our kids to be robust and bold. We want to see them lead lives of following Jesus and making a significant difference in the world. We desire for them to care about the things Jesus cares about: the poor, the sick, the needy, and the spiritually lost.

But in a lot of cases, that's not happening. In fact, we are living in a time in history where we are seeing less and less connection to Jesus. Churches are shrinking and closing their doors. Students are walking away from their faith in college, and many don't seem to be finding their way back.

And we parents are a big part of the problem. We are unintentionally passing on a faith that is weak. We aren't happy about it, but if we take a long look at our own current faith story, we might have to admit that we are not pleased with where we are. But it's more than just us, right? We are part of churches—some of which are trying really hard to pass on faith, but it's not working and we are seeing a decline.

In this section we will look at six different problems that shape why we are not passing on bold faith to our kids. Because you're probably like me—busy running around all over the place trying to love and care for your kids—I'm going to write out the problems as simply as I can make them. I'm going to leave out a lot of facts and figures. That's often how I want to read: I just want the problems identified simply, and I care more about coming up with solutions—not because the facts and figures aren't important, but because I don't want them to slow me down as I read. But if you want a deeper understanding of the data and info behind problems, the appendix at the end of this book includes a list of additional resources that can help you.

It's important for you to understand that I certainly have my struggles as a parent. As a dad of three kids—ages 12, 10, and 8—I often find myself getting stuck in the world of finances, business, and control. I lose sight of Jesus and how I should be living, and instead try to grab tightly to the things I can manage and try to lead in that way. Fortunately, I have some great friends who have really modeled what it means to follow Jesus with their families. I'm not going to say that I have this figured out at all, but I will admit that writing this book has been a huge help to me because it has pushed me to grow.

CHAPTER 1
OUR CHURCHES AREN'T BOLD ENOUGH

I grew up in a mainline denominational church. Recently I drove past it to show my kids where I spent so much time as a child and in middle and high school ministry. As we drove by, they said, "It's so small." My wife and I talked later about how I remember it not having a lot of life. She remarked about the number of times she's heard me say that I didn't really learn about Jesus there. Sadly, it's true. Yes, the church had some really great people who impacted me in a lot of ways, but I don't remember having any sort of significant conversation with anyone about Jesus. On top of that, there also really wasn't much space for any action. We did camp and retreats but had little to no focus on service, mission, or projects aimed at helping others or sharing our faith.

What kind of church did you grow up in—or what kind of church did you attend when you came to faith in Christ as a teenager or an adult? Maybe you have stories of how your church had a significant impact on your spiritual growth. I know many people have had these kinds of experiences. But do those experiences lead to lasting life-change? Are our churches leading people to a place of bold faith where they follow in the footsteps of Jesus and do the things he did?

FOCUSING ON THE WRONG THINGS

Over the years I've spent a large amount of time with many different churches. My early years of ministry had me working at a camp for four summers and multiple winters. In that role I interacted with hundreds of youth leaders, pastors, and congregations. I had the opportunity to get to know some really great people, but unfortunately, I heard far too many stories of churches that were literally falling apart around them. Additionally, I've worked in five churches that would be described as "mega" (more than 2,000 members). A lot of great things happened in those churches, but I don't think I would categorize them as "bold."

Yes, there will always be bold individuals within most churches, but what about the church as a whole? Too many congregations focus big chunks of their energy and attention on the worship styles, budgets, people in the seats, the happiness of members, paint schemes, parking lot, and other things that aren't related to building and living a bold faith. That sounds harsh, but it's the reality that I see in too many churches today.

Do many churches passionately and boldly love Jesus? Of course! In fact, I serve at a church now that is a bold church filled with people who collectively and individually love Jesus. With that said, though, my church belongs to a denomination that is literally falling apart around us—a denomination that is not bold. I believe my denomination has lost sight of so much of its roots and the work of Jesus—and it has begun to focus so much of its energy on everything else that it has lost the ability to be bold.

I wish that I had more hope for our churches right now. Some of them are really great ones doing cool things that are helping the congregations to grow, but unfortunately, many churches are dying or close to it.

FINDING BOLD CHURCHES IN ACTION

What does it look like when a church is living boldly? Here's an example: My current church has a ministry that was started with the sole purpose of impacting the local schools. In its early phase, the ministry's goal was to create a program for students across the street from a middle school. But after they got up and running (which took a ton of prayer, bold faith, and belief from some donors, volunteers, pastors, and members), the organizers quickly realized that they needed to do more than just this drop-in center.

Through conversations with the middle school principal, they were asked to come on campus and start an after-school program. Long story short, that ministry now leads the after-school sports programs at all five local middle schools. And just recently, I heard stories about how gang activity had diminished significantly and test scores were shooting up in crazy ways. These are the things that happen when a church or a ministry is committed to taking bold steps and demonstrating bold faith.

Sadly, though, I don't think the overall church culture in the United States is overflowing with this type of story. In fact, within our society today, churches are often known more for what we are against and less for what we are doing. And as a longtime youth pastor, I could share story after story of kids who appeared to have strong faith in their middle and high school years but who quickly shelved it and walked away from their faith after graduation.

The reality is that people are the church, and when a congregation isn't bold, it is generally a reflection of the people who attend. In the next chapter we will take a look at Christians and some of the problems of our lack of boldness.

THINK ABOUT:

1. What stories of boldness have you witnessed in your own church—or in other congregations?

2. How have you participated in something bold at your church? How did that experience impact you?

3. If you had to list three specific areas in your life, in your family, or in your congregation where boldness is lacking, what would be on that list?

4. Take time to pray for those three things and ask God to help your church to become bolder.

CHAPTER 2

WE CHRISTIANS AREN'T BOLD ENOUGH

Far too often, Christians don't look, act, think, or respond differently than non-Christians do. Something tells me that isn't how God wants it to be.

Think about the last time you were at church or hanging out with a bunch of other Christians. If a non-Christian were there with you, how might that person know that the people around you were Christians? Now make it one step more personal. How well could a non-Christian tell that *you* are a Christian?

Imagine if this friend spent a day following you around and observing everything you do. What would lead this person to believe that you live your life differently? Do you regularly care for the poor? Are you compassionate? Do the Fruit of the Spirit—such as patience, love, peace, kindness, gentleness, self-control—drip off of you? Maybe you're like me and you have moments when you do really well and are living in a Christlike way, but you also have those moments when you fail to really live into what it means to be a follower of Jesus.

This goes far beyond looking physically different from a non-Christian. I don't think God wants us to have a special haircut or a rotation of Christian T-shirts to set us apart from the world. But in the ways that it truly matters, often there is very little in many Christians' lives that really marks us as different.

TAKING A PEEK INSIDE

One of my favorite images to explain this reality is a red Solo® cup. One night I was standing outside in Austin, Texas, surrounded by thousands of other people. Everywhere I looked, I saw red cups (and cowboy boots, of course), and I found myself thinking about the people represented there. Everyone looked the same, and it was virtually impossible to distinguish anything about anyone from the outside. Like a "red Solo cup," we all looked the same regardless of what was going on the inside.

As a "cup" that looks the same on the outside as a million other "cups," we each can blend in with society—there doesn't seem to be anything that sets us apart. Yes, we may be different and what's inside us may be lined up with the heart of Jesus, but how often do people get to see it? Sadly, I think that many of us Christians have decided that segmenting our lives into different areas makes things work more easily. So we can be a Christian and act like Christ in settings where it makes sense—church, Bible studies, at small groups, or when we are serving. But it's so easy to put that faith on a shelf when we are in other settings such as sporting events, out to dinner, with our kids, or at work.

I'm a dad who spends a lot of time with my kids in public settings. I've been known to be impatient, and sometimes I don't say or do the right thing. I know that it's OK as a Christian to fail and stumble, but shouldn't I be living differently? Shouldn't I wear my faith on my sleeve a little bit more than I do? I really wish more people would regularly ask me, "Something's different about you—what is it?" That would open the door to talking about Jesus and sharing why my faith is an important part of my life. Sadly, I don't get asked that question often enough.

THINK ABOUT:

1. What evidence would you expect to see in the life of a Christian who's living boldly?

2. What are some differences between living boldly for Christ and living weirdly for Christ?

3. Why do many Christians not look or live much differently than non-Christians?

CHAPTER 3

NARROW PARENTAL FAITH HINDERS BOLD LIVING

Sometimes I wonder if my faith is solid and bold enough that I can be proud to share it with my kids. Yes, I'm a pastor and I know that I'm supposed to have it all together, but it's essential that I'm honest as I write. You see, I worry that my faith is weak. I worry that I don't trust God enough and that ultimately I'm teaching my kids that the American dream is just as important as faith in Jesus.

I'm not sure when it happened for many of us parents. I remember when I was 23: I was living for Jesus and had a very strong faith journey. I was praying all the time, and going to church and college group. Bible studies were a big part of my life, and I was serving regularly, too. But then something happened and my focus began to slowly shift away toward taking care of my family and myself. It was a slow process (maybe slower because I was a pastor), but as all my friends and I got older, it just seemed on some level that the flame started to diminish.

KEEPING GOD BIG AND BOLD

I used to tell my youth group students that a bigger view of God really helped when you were dealing with problems. When God is big, problems appear little. I'm not sure what has happened as I've gotten older, but it seems my problems have gotten a bit bigger. Does that mean my God has gotten smaller?

Many of us parents have narrowly defined our faith walk and connection to God to the times that we are in the physical church building. We connect with our faith on Sunday mornings and maybe during the week, if we attend a Bible study or small group. We too easily lose sight of our faith as it applies to everyday life. A narrow faith is one that limits God and what he can do.

I'm ashamed to admit that I recently had a discussion (read "argument") with my wife during which I was narrowing down the things God cared about, and she reminded me that Jesus cares about birds. Wow, what a zinger from someone who has a much deeper and bolder faith than I do! She was right, of course, that God cares about way more in our lives than I give him credit for—and that my limiting God's role in our lives was part of the problem with my living a bold faith.

EXAMINING OUR OWN PATTERNS

I sometimes wonder why my kids don't do a better job of expressing their faith at school, with their friends, and in other areas of day-to-day life. But when I point the finger at myself instead of at my kids, I realize that I am guilty of the same thing. This past week I've been at a variety of social settings where I could or should have been wearing my faith more on my sleeve (meaning just being transparent about the things that matter) but I didn't, and I wasn't a very bold example of a parent with faith.

Parenting is hard. We have so many competing priorities for our kids. We have school, sports, extracurricular activities, and more.

Along the way, we have to make frequent choices about how we prioritize our time. I wonder if you are like me and faith isn't always the highest priority.

Please understand that I realize bold parenting isn't always easy. But I will offer some specific, practical steps and suggestions in the third section of this book—steps that can help us reflect Jesus in all we do.

THINK ABOUT:

1. Where and when do you struggle most at being bold in your faith as a parent?

2. What are some examples of truly bold faith you've demonstrated as a parent?

3. What specific changes might you make right now that could help your faith become deeper?

4. How might having a deeper and bolder faith change the way you parent? Think of some specific ways.

CHAPTER 4

MORALISM ISN'T CHRISTIANITY

I believe very strongly that there are particular ways we need to live as a Christian. However, I also believe that we have created a version of Christianity that is all about moralism and "doing right"—and that has become our view about what God wants. The truth is far from that. As Dallas Willard wrote in his book *The Divine Conspiracy*, the gospel of sin management is really no gospel at all. [1]

RAISING MORE THAN SOBER VIRGINS

My earliest suggestion for this book's title was *SoberVirgins: There Has to Be More to Faith*. We realized that some bookstores might be uncomfortable with that title and that some parents might be unsure of my message, but it still sticks with me as the best way to describe this chapter. Picture a boy sitting in a pew and looking uncomfortable in a suit, appearing as sad as possible. He is "doing" the right things morally and is both sober and celibate—but miserable.

Now don't me wrong: I think there are significant, healthy, moral ways we ought to live, but too many of us have ascribed moralism to Christianity and limited it almost entirely to that. In other words, we've redefined Christianity to be just about behavior that we consider moral, right, and appropriate.

And while some parts of moralism are right and consistent with leading a Jesus-centered life, as a whole when we narrow faith down to simple moralism, we have lost the gospel.

Think about it from this perspective. You are at a church where the pastor is preaching a sermon about "good Christian living" and you hear about the things we are supposed to do: refrain from or limit our consumption of alcohol; no sex with anyone you aren't married to; don't lie, cheat, or steal. It's a "Ten Commandments Plus" sermon aimed at getting you to follow the values of the Bible.

But then you start thinking about the times in your life when you have blown it. You've done some (or a lot) of the things that the pastor is saying are against the Christian faith. Now imagine being a child or student, and you've just messed up in a big way for the first time. It's easy to see why students begin to pull away from the Christian faith if we say it's all about moralism. They feel rejected by a church that says, "Here are the standards—live by them and don't mess up. And if you do mess up, we will look down upon you because you have failed to live by the 'Christian Moral Code.' "

CREATING STRUGGLES FOR OUR KIDS

As a youth pastor, it was always easy to see when students began to walk down the slippery slope (or sometimes run quickly) of leaving the church because they felt their lifestyle was too incompatible with faith. They couldn't figure out how to justify their actions on Saturday night with the message that they were getting from the church on Sunday mornings.

It was less about grace, mercy, and forgiveness and more about rules and right living.

Now don't misunderstand me. There are great reasons why we should live in a particular way, and living morally isn't wrong. We want to train our kids in the way they should go so that they don't depart from it (see Proverbs 22:6). But we have to broaden our conversations about this because right now, society believes the Christian church is so focused on morality and the "right way to live" that anyone who has struggled or is living the wrong way is rejected and not invited to the table.

We need to be more about what we are "for" and not always about what we are "against." God is about grace, love, mercy, forgiveness, and hope. We fail when we decide that moralism is the most important thing and that we are going to ascribe God merely characteristics as the judge of how we should be living.

THINK ABOUT:

1. When have you equated Christianity with moralism, and how did that affect your faith journey?

2. When you have blown it, how have you experienced the church still loving you? How have you been rejected?

3. How can we share the essential "do's and don'ts" of faith with our children without it becoming moralism or legalism?

CHAPTER 5
GOD ISN'T A THERAPIST

Before I go any further, I should state that I like therapists. I've been to some good ones, and they are often helpful in walking me through a journey of growth and discovery. With that said, I think one reason our faith isn't bold is that we have put God into the box of being our therapist that we can interact with when we need help. The rest of the time, we just handle things on our own.

CHOOSING HOW WE SEE GOD

This mentality feeds the habit of reaching out to God only when we really need him. The picture that I see is of a student who's praying that God will step in and meet his or her needs because that's what God does. God is simply waiting around for us to ask and then steps in to solve our problems—but the rest of the time he is off doing his own thing.

When we have a view of God being the cosmic therapist in our lives, we miss out on having a real and open relationship with God that helps us as we go throughout the day. God as therapist reduces God from being omniscient, omnipresent, and omnipotent to simply being at our beck and call when we need him.

When we pass on to our children a faith that puts God in the role of therapist, we do them a disservice because we narrow and minimize the role God ought to have—and wants to have—in their lives. And this model of bringing God out of the box when we need him makes it easier to walk away from faith. Students can put God back in the box anytime they want. This seems to really happen when they leave our homes. Whether they're heading to college, the military, or the workforce, if they head out with the belief that God is simply a therapist, they can easily take a step away from him, intending just to come back "when it's time" or "when God is needed." The sad reality is that more and more of them seem to be leaving God in the box and not coming back.

ASSIGNING GOD THE WRONG ROLE

I think God cares about us and does want to meet our needs. But I think we all sometimes limit his power and role in our lives, and that makes our faith so weak, small, and diminished compared with what it could really be. It's not a bold faith when we become more powerful or try to limit God.

I love the scene from *The Lion, the Witch and the Wardrobe* when Lucy asks about whether or not Aslan the lion—the Christ figure in this series of books and movies—is safe. The answer she gets is that he isn't safe but he is good.[2] If we assign God the role of therapist, we don't allow him to be a part of "all" of our lives—or even to "mess up" our lives. Instead, we are simply allowing God to participate when we need some cosmic therapy that will help us wade through our problems right at that moment.

And when we teach our kids that God is a therapist, we expose them to a faith without teeth. This God in his sweater and loafers doesn't really impact our lives outside of the walls of his therapist office. God isn't engaged with us every day, but instead just when we are at church or just when we remember that he exists. But that isn't an accurate view of God at all.

THINK ABOUT:

1. How have you seen the idea of God as therapist in your own life or in other people's lives?

2. How might you be unintentionally teaching this to your kids?

3. What are some steps you can take for God to be more than a therapist in your own life—and in the lives of your children?

CHAPTER 6
GOD DIDN'T WALK AWAY

I think an awful lot of us today wonder what's up with God. If we're 100 percent honest, we'd admit that we often struggle with understanding what God is up to—or if God even exists. That's why deism is an easy trap to fall into. It's easy to conclude that it had to take a God to create things because all the intricate creatures and plants and systems of this world—including humans—couldn't and didn't just happen by chance. But after that, we wonder if he's even involved anymore. And at its root, that's what deism is: an absentee God who isn't engaged with us after he set it all up.

REJECTING A DEIST WORLDVIEW

It's hard to develop and demonstrate bold faith when we view God as uninvolved. But it's easy to see why so many young people have this type of faith. It's what they've seen modeled and displayed by parents and peers—and sometimes even by pastors. In fact, Kenda Creasy Deen in her book *Almost Christian* says that the main reason children and students have this type of faith is because we as parents model it to them.[3]

Deism declares that God isn't involved and doesn't have a role in our lives today. It fits really well with Western thought because we are so often taught that our success depends on our own hard work. This is, in part, why we put so much pressure and concern into what we do and how we do it. Children have private coaches and tutors as young as preschool to ensure that they will have an edge in beating out others so that they will be more successful in life. Young athletes are told to set their sights on success at the collegiate and professional levels. Academically minded students feel depressed and defeated when just one B appears on their report card. Too many people—including Christians—have bought into the lie that God doesn't care about us and is just not actively involved in the world or our individual lives.

I'm Presbyterian by church background, and one thing that characterizes us is that we generally have a small view of the Trinity. It's almost as if we forget that the Holy Spirit exists and has a role today in the world and in our lives. If the living, breathing Spirit of God isn't active in our faith, we lose sight that God is up to something now. This is part of the problem with the church I grew up in, too. We weren't raised to believe in the active role of God, and that perspective shaped our faith.

EXAMINING OUR VIEW OF GOD

Much of what we do as parents shapes how our kids see God, and this is one of those areas where I probably need to confess that I struggle. I'm a hard worker who—even now while sitting at Starbucks® writing this manuscript—worries about my deadline and if it will even be good enough to publish. I find myself agonizing over the words of this book more than the prayers that I should be saying as I write it. I sometimes think that even in the things I'm working on the most, I may be moving in my own direction and not the way God would have me go. I think back to the moment the publisher gave me the green light to write this, and my first thought is "thank you,

God" because I knew that it was only because of God and his plan that I was going to become a writer. But that was several months ago, and now I'm sitting and writing and wondering how much my view of God needs to change.

Deism paves the way for a lot of false ideas about faith. It's hard to live boldly if we don't believe that God is a part of what we are doing. It's easy to simply take a step back and put it all on our shoulders, which requires almost no faith at all. If we teach this view of God, we can't guide our kids toward a faith that is bold. Instead, we share a faith that starts and ends with us—a faith that can't get bigger than our own views, ideas, and dreams.

When explaining these ideas to a teenager, I'll often talk about driving a car. I'll simply ask the student to imagine being in a car as it's moving down the road. Jesus is in the car with the teenager, I say, but then I'll ask what he would be doing. I get a variety of answers, but the most common one is that Jesus is sitting in the passenger seat and is along for the ride as the "co-pilot." Occasionally a student will say, "Jesus is driving and I'm just enjoying it" but the predominate answer reveals that the teenager believes he or she is in charge and God just happens to be along for the ride. That is an accurate picture of deism. God isn't active and involved, and if he wasn't there we could just do it alone. This is a false view of God.

THINK ABOUT:

1. How often do you wonder what God is up to in the world?

2. Do you believe a deistic view ever creeps into how you parent your kids? If so, how?

3. What role does the Holy Spirit have in your faith journey?

4. What are a couple of steps you could take that would expand your view of God beyond deism?

PART 2:
KNOWING WHAT OUR KIDS REALLY NEED

This stuff in this next section is way more fun to discuss than the problems in Part 1. Now I get the chance to share some things that I have seen to be true during my 20+ years of working with kids, teenagers, and families. I have encountered and examined a number of things that I believe young people need in order to have bold faith and to move beyond a Christian journey that is all about following rules.

I hope that the stories of boldness that I share will encourage you to seek out and find ways of living into similar stories. My goal is to give you opportunities to live into a faith journey that models all of it because, as I have said, your own journey of bold faith is the best and most effective way to teach your own kids how to have bold faith.

In this section, we'll look at how our children need opportunities to cultivate bold faith in their lives. We will see how being connected to a bold church will help them to be active and engaged in their faith journey. You will read again and again how your role is so important and why your own bold faith is crucial to helping your children grow.

We'll also evaluate the Christian culture and examine the importance of giving our kids the opportunity to experience a bold culture that can impact and grow the world around them. Lastly, we will look at how our children can gain a bold view of who God is and how that might impact the way they respond to your dreams and goals for them. Consider all of this a starting point for you to see what your kids need in their faith journey!

Because we will be talking about things that young people need to see in us, these topics might make you anxious, discouraged, or frustrated. But I pray and hope you can make it through to Part 3 of this book, where you will discover practical steps to helping your kids have bold faith.

CHAPTER 7
BOLD FAITH

Kids and teenagers need to have "bold faith" defined for them. I define it as "living for and with Jesus." It's something that they learn and grow into best as they see older adults in their lives doing it. It's why adults who love Jesus are so important in the lives of our children. Think about a young child who wants to be a firefighter, a doctor, a teacher, or an artist—that child mimics and picks up on the traits of people. If we put older people in their lives who are modeling bold faith, then they are more likely to take on those characteristics.

DEFINING A FOLLOWER OF JESUS

In many ways, our kids have the ability to be more successful at living a bold faith than we are as adults. Their lives are not yet so burdened. Their worldview is still developing. They can try new things and take risks that might be difficult for adults to do.

A number of years ago I was on a mission trip in Vancouver, British Columbia. We had been serving in a homeless shelter for most of the day and caring for a variety of different men. That night we were told that we were going to go out on the streets and pray for prostitutes and pass out roses. I was immediately terrified about this experience. I was a 20-something youth pastor who would have to explain to parents why I was taking their 14-year-old sons to talk to prostitutes. I was so uncomfortable thinking about it that I determined that when we went out walking that night,

I would simply lead us away from where I knew all the prostitutes were hanging out so we wouldn't have to interact with them. Great bold faith, right?

Well, that evening I followed my plan, but after a while my group figured out that we weren't in the right spot. They told me we needed to go to another area, so I begrudgingly led them in that direction. When we got there, one young student in my group said, "Let's pray and see who God wants us to give our rose to." We prayed and then started walking. Almost immediately, that same student saw a woman standing in a doorway and said, "That's her." We went over and he engaged her in a brief conversation before asking if we could pray for her—and then he gave her the rose. As we walked away, I thought about how much of a weak faith I had at that moment, even as a youth pastor, and how I needed this young man named Roark to point me toward solid, bold faith.

ENCOUNTERING THE DIVINE

Another story: Some years back, I took more than 100 students on a houseboat trip in Arizona. As part of our program one night, we ran more than 200 feet of extension cords onto the top of a plateau where the worship band set up. Our evening meeting was the most amazing worship experience I have ever been a part of. Here we were in the middle of nowhere, on top of a mountain with a full sound system and band, and students were singing their hearts out and worshipping God.

There were no lights, so we could see the amazing Milky Way. Then off in the distance a lightning storm started. It was so evident and clear that God was powerful and in control at that moment. The way the students responded with unhindered singing and worship was incredibly bold. Even now, 10 years later, I still have conversations with students about how that night really taught them about worship.

For faith to stay strong and real, it has to be bold. Something that is weak and lacking excitement or passion will not last—that's sort of a no-brainer. Imagine how students feel when they show up to an event or gathering where we are talking about God and faith—if we are sharing it in a way that makes it seem uninspiring and unexciting, it seems only natural that many would walk away completely disinterested in God.

STEPPING AWAY TO FOCUS ON GOD

One of the benefits of retreats for kids or teenagers is the opportunity to pull them outside of their normal life for a week or weekend and give them time to focus on God. In my current church, the first major retreat we do with students happens right after fifth grade. We take them away for four nights to a local camp and surround them with leaders who love Jesus, have bold faith, and demonstrate a strong desire to pass that faith on to the students. The focus and goal of that week is for these young people to have their faith become "more real" to them. When it becomes more real, it becomes bolder, and we have seen time and time again that a bold faith is a lasting faith.

These are examples from my world of church ministry. But we as parents also can give our children opportunities to learn about what it means to have a bold faith. You can serve as a family. You can give as a family. You can take risks as a family. Look for simple opportunities in your daily routines. Or get truly bold and go on a mission trip as a family.

THINK ABOUT:

1. What things are your children doing that could help them establish a bolder faith?

2. How much boldness do you see in your children's faith right now? Try to identify specific examples.

3. What things from your life have contributed to you having a bold faith—or to having a weak faith?

CHAPTER 8
BOLD CHURCHES

Our children need to see a bold church. The church, of course, is not the building but the people who are followers of Jesus, so what I'm saying here is that our kids need to see boldness displayed by a collection of Christ-followers who gather together. Young people need to see boldness modeled by pastors, teachers, elders, janitors, volunteers, people sitting in the pew, and everyone else who's part of what the church does. This boldness needs to be reflected in bulletins, posters, videos, songs, and sermons. Our children need to be inundated with the message that the church is really a living, breathing mass of people boldly following Jesus.

FIGURING OUT THE CHURCH'S ROLE

One of my former senior pastors was a huge proponent of getting to know people outside of the church walls. He liked to spend a lot of time at a place where surfers congregated—and he even had a specific bench where he usually sat. Invariably, he would strike up conversations with people who were watching the waves, and the discussion almost always led to "what do you do?" He said that question brought a little bit of fear but also gave him a great opportunity to talk about Jesus. That's a bold pastor.

In my current church, we offer two different types of worship styles. And what's great is there really isn't any conflict between the services. We all sort of agree that God is up to something and that these particular styles of worship are reaching people where they are. Everyone gets along and has decided that they are going to believe in what the other service is doing. That's bold, because so many churches endure wars over worship styles.

Want to talk really bold? Just a few weeks ago our church and many other churches on the east side of Lake Washington shut their doors on a Sunday. The day before, about 25 churches had come together to serve in the community. We helped set up several middle and elementary schools to start the new school year. People helped with painting, weeding, sharpening pencils, digging, and more—all because these churches came together and said they wanted to make a difference. And then on Sunday we shut our facilities' doors and all showed up at a local park in downtown Bellevue for worship. It was amazing.

APPRECIATING BOLD CONGREGATIONS

Not all kids and teenagers would recognize how bold of a step this was, but you and I can appreciate that it was huge. These churches said that they would give up being together in their own little kingdom for a weekend and come together with others. It was huge to give up on doing an offering for one Sunday—especially for my church, which was about to end its fiscal year. And at the service, no one on the stage mentioned what church they were from. "We" literally had become one big church for a Sunday in a park. That was so bold.

Our children need to see us making these kinds of decisions. They need to see that we follow Jesus and truly care about the things he cares about. When we get caught up in insignificant issues that we make into major obstacles, or when we focus on things that really don't matter, we do a disservice to our young people, who need us to be bold.

THINK ABOUT:

1. What bold things is your church doing? How have you participated?

2. How have your children experienced the church being bold? How does it affect them?

3. What are some things that you could envision your church doing that would be bold and would model a great faith to your kids? How could you help turn those ideas into reality?

CHAPTER 9
BOLD PARENTS

I have a friend named Phil. He's a dad with three girls, and he's been married almost the exact same amount of time as me. Phil is a missionary with Youth With a Mission and is my hero. I met him on a mission trip over 10 years ago, and we became really good friends. We have a lot in common because of our love of God, our desire for students to have a lasting relationship with Jesus, and our focus on wanting to model a faith journey for our kids that is real, lasting, and bold.

Phil lives a completely different story from me, and honestly I am envious about his relationship with God. Many times in our friendship I have been on the receiving end of Phil sharing where he feels the Holy Spirit leading him and his family and how he desires to be in God's will as he leads and cares for people. Just this summer he led two major trips to Cambodia aimed at impacting many people's faith and caring for a country that has gone through so much pain. When I look at Phil's life, I see someone who is modeling the right kind of bold faith.

ENDURING SPIRITUAL SELF-EXAMINATION

Then I look at my own journey. I'm a pastor so I know that counts for something, but I find myself wishing that I was living a more sold-out and exciting life for Jesus. I wish I were bolder with my faith—both in how I tell others what I do and in the way that I trust God to lead me. I know comparison is wrong, but it just feels like Phil has it way more figured out than me.

But I also know God has me where he does for a purpose. I know that writing this book and being so transparent will be eye-opening for some people who know me and who read this. Maybe God has me exactly where I am for the sole purpose of ripping the veil off of the life of being a pastor, because my honesty will be transformative for some people who have me up on an ivory tower because of my ecclesial status.

As parents, we have the opportunity to demonstrate a faith that's filled with purpose, and our children need to see how that plays out. I've been around amazing dads who work in major companies who share about the Bible studies they lead or the prayer times they are a part of. I've seen the same people consistently inviting others to church. They have come up with a plan for how they want to live out their faith—and they are actively, consistently doing it.

BECOMING A FAMILY ROLE MODEL

Children need to see that we have a faith that is, at least in part, figured out. They need to see us with a plan that shows we know a little bit about what we are doing. My wife and I talk about the word *consistency* a lot. Kids and teenagers need to see that we are consistent in our faith journey—that we are reliable and that our faith isn't just something we are into for a little bit and then something else takes its place. When we are inconsistent and not modeling a healthy and reliable faith, young people begin to wonder if it's all real or not. We need to show them through our lives and actions that it is real.

Modeling bold faith also requires that we avoid the path of hypocrisy. This is similar to consistency but a little different—we can be consistent and still be hypocrites who do one thing at home and another at church. As a pastor, this is an area that I think about a lot. At church I'm a smiling, welcoming face, but I struggle to maintain the same demeanor in my own home. And my kids fully get it. They know when dad is "putting on a show" at church but resorts back to being impatient and not careful with his words at home. For me to have a bold faith of my own, I have to work hard at making sure my life lines up so that what I say I believe and how I come across at church line up with who I am when I am home.

Children also need to know that you can answer questions about faith. (It helps if you can answer other questions, too, of course!) You don't have to have all the answers figured out—just some of the basic answers (or at least know where to find them). I have a son who loves to ask questions, and if I constantly said, "I don't know" to his questions, he would probably really doubt that my faith was real to me.

Our kids also need to see that our faith models grace and forgiveness. This is a big one for me because I often feel like I need those things from people in my life. But it's more than just needing grace and forgiveness—it's about offering them, too. We need to be people who model a faith filled with love, truth, forgiveness, honesty, and grace. When our children see us doing these things, it can build into them a deeper faith that has roots in Jesus and the way he lived.

THINK ABOUT:

1. What are the most important parts of your faith journey right now? Why?

2. On a scale of 1-10 (with a 10 as highest), how satisfied are you with your walk with Jesus? Why did you give yourself that particular score?

3. What obstacles stand in the way of your faith journey growing and deepening?

4. How important do you believe your own faith journey is to your kids' faith? Why?

CHAPTER 10
BOLD CULTURE

One common struggle facing our young people is deciding how the Jesus they believe in can interact with their world and culture on a day-to-day basis. Where they seem to struggle the most is the artificial wall between their "Christian" culture and the culture of the world. I can't tell you the number of times I have heard teenagers refer to "church friends" as a completely different group from their "school friends." They have created a separation in their mind and in a physical space between their faith journey and the culture they live in. Except, of course, where those things intersects, and that can get messy.

UNDERSTANDING HOW CHRIST AND CULTURE INTERACT

Oftentimes we in the church unintentionally set up the expectations that distinct differences and incongruities exist between "Culture" and "Christ." That's why many people in the church believe we must co-opt culture and make it our own. Have you ever seen (or perhaps even bought) Testamints® or the myriad Christian T-shirts that proclaim slogans strikingly similar to branding done by major companies? I almost gagged the first time I saw a "Jesus: The Real Thing" T-shirt that looked like the Coca-Cola® slogan. The number of shirts with knockoff candy bar or "Whatsssupppp????? (it's Jesus that's up)" slogans makes me sad. All of these had the purpose of trying to grab something culturally relevant to young people and bring it into church, but I think largely they failed.

We can proclaim a message of following Jesus that is bold. We don't have to shy away from it. If we are truly living an exciting life of following Jesus where he would have us go, then it is not boring. Caring for people, believing that God is in charge, loving those who culture says are unlovable, standing up for things that are right—all of these things are exciting and can be shown as bold. What isn't bold is putting on a suit for church and going and sitting in a pew the whole time looking at your watch ready to go to lunch. That's the kind of faith action that is literally killing our children's faith.

A bunch of years back, a couple of my friends decided to start a skateboard company. At the time, this industry was very dark and had a lot of disturbing images on boards and T-shirts. They decided to call their company "Renaissance," and its goal was to simply bring back some great imagery and artwork from that time period. Both guys were strong Christians, and they created something with significant art appeal. It was done well and had a solid influence on the local skater community. They didn't go in trying to just take the logos the kids were already wearing and "make" them Christian. They just took something that was already a part of our history and used it. It was already cool—they just brought it back.

CHOOSING TO INFLUENCE CULTURE

I lived and worked near Los Angeles for about eight years. During that time I had ongoing interaction with friends who were involved in the entertainment industry—and were also Christians. It was significant to see how they went about living their faith in Jesus while also being a part of an industry that's all about shaping culture. And I'm proud to say that my friends were part of some great examples of movies that were made— and not made! But it was dark, too. I know that there were plenty of Christians trying to "make it" who had to wrestle with what parts they'd take or what projects they would be a part of as they struggled to make ends meet.

The best way to explain to our young people how to be a Christian in culture is to say that we can be bold in bringing Christ to the world if the journey we are walking is bold. We don't have to try to take the world and change its messages, but we also don't have to be all about the world. We can pursue a balance between what we can do as followers of Christ and how we love and care for culture without getting lost in it. Young people need to see that Jesus can have a voice in things that happen on MTV or in a football stadium. They need to see that Jesus cares about people who are making questionable choices and living lives that are completely opposite of what God desires. We can speak truth and love and grace and mercy to culture without simply rejecting it.

THINK ABOUT:

1. What are some places where you have figured out how your Christian faith and culture can interact well?

2. Are there areas of culture where you just don't know how to best interact as a follower of Jesus? Why or why not?

3. How can you model to your children healthy yet bold interactions with culture?

CHAPTER 11

BOLD UNDERSTANDING OF GOD

Our children need to be free of those false views of God that I discussed earlier in the book: the moralistic, therapeutic, or deist God. Unfortunately, this view is so pervasive. It's all around us and continues to shape how we do things inside and outside of the church. When young people feel that God is shaped in this direction, it certainly doesn't make their God seem bold.

A bold God is a living, breathing, exciting God. God is active and engaged in the world today. God cares about even small things like sparrows. God is like a roaring lion and also a rushing wind. God is moving and real and close by. The words *omniscient*, *omnipotent*, and *omnipresent* describe who he is— he is all-knowing, all-powerful, and present everywhere.

LOOKING FOR THE RIGHT PIECES

Our kids need to see this kind of active God because they are deeply attuned to foundations. Children sometimes understand how things work much better than adults do. We adults have learned to fudge a little. We think if we do one thing in a particular way, we can "get away with"—even if we don't do it exactly the way it should be done. Children are less savvy and more concrete. If a block doesn't fit upon another block, then it likely doesn't go there. When things don't fit together, such as puzzles, they just look for the right pieces.

Adults want to just make things work, which can end up shaping the kind of faith we model for our kids.

I shared earlier that children don't have the hang-ups that adults often do. If God doesn't heal someone, kids are generally OK with believing that it wasn't God's will or timing. That itself is a bold statement because they realize that God isn't about our timing and plans. And it doesn't mess them up quite so much when God doesn't answer a prayer.

We have to create opportunities for them to see that God is boldly active in the world today. Again, this is the reason we need to get them out of their comfort zones and see the world. I recently took a group of high school students to Costa Rica. While there, they met Pastor Jorge, who believed so strongly that God could dream bigger than he did that he and his church decided their dream of creating a community center, day care, and orphanage in the neighborhood was attainable.

They had no money and just a few grandmas and Pastor Jorge to pray. So that's what they did. They asked God that they would be aligned with his will. They questioned their dreams and prayed that if God wanted those dreams to be reality, he would make them happen. And those hopes did become a reality—but the answers to prayer went above and beyond the dreams they had. When Pastor Jorge shared that story with our students, they got a great picture of a bold understanding of God and what he can do.

HELPING OUR KIDS LIVE BOLDLY

If our children believe in a bold God, they can live differently. They won't be stuck in fear or worry that they are outside of God's will. They will know what God is up to and will want to be a part of it. They can dream big dreams—or what I like to call "God-sized dreams" that are above and beyond anything we could even imagine. "Oh, you want to care for a few followers? How about I feed 5,000 people with a few loaves and some fish?" What? How can that happen?

Passing along a bold understanding of God means we have to instill in our children a solid understanding of the Bible—what it means, why it's vital to our lives, and how to follow its truths. It requires us as parents, teachers, and adults to teach young people that fully understanding God involves studying him and seeing what he is up to. Looking for bold "God sightings" should be fun. The reality is that they are often all around us. I see a bold God every Thursday when I run into Mike, who comes and prays with our pastoral staff. Mike is a retired man who has an incredible bold faith in God. His life models an active and exciting God who is so far beyond the moralistic, therapeutic, deist God that many people follow today.

THINK ABOUT:

1. What traps do you fall into that can limit your view of God as bold?

2. In order to pass on to your children a faith that reveals an active and bold God, how might you need to change the way you act?

3. When in your life has your view of God as bold been the strongest?

CHAPTER 12
BOLD EXPECTATIONS AND DREAMS

What happens when the faith of our kids is stronger than our own? What do we do when our children push us to grow and challenge us to realize that we are living a weak faith? How do we respond when they have different visions and dreams than we have? How do we cultivate a faith in them that says they are to follow Jesus first before they simply follow our plans for them?

Those are tough questions, aren't they?

SETTING THE RIGHT EXPECTATIONS

I love the idea of "bold expectations," and I'm convinced young people are just better at comprehending this than we are. We seem to have the great ability to limit God and what he can do by ascribing to him too many of our own characteristics. We know what we are capable of and assume that God has those same kinds of limits. But our young people are not hindered by our limitations. They believe the Bible accounts that God can blow down walls with trumpets, that Jesus can raise the dead and heal the sick. They don't have a problem with the feeding of the 5,000 or walking on water.

Because they are so attuned to these things that God can do, they have the ability to set some bold expectations and believe in bold dreams. And our job is to help them as they travel this path of bold faith.

Years ago, a student in my youth group believed God was telling him he needed to interact with people who were homeless in Santa Monica, California. But this teenager didn't want to just pass out food—he wanted to build friendships with them. I volunteered to help him, and the way we initially were going to do this was through food. We set up around some tables outside a fast-food restaurant, and when a homeless person walked by we would engage them in conversation.

Things didn't get off to a solid start: Just about 15 minutes into this, one of the homeless guys dumped an entire large soda on my head. Needless to say, I was less optimistic that my student's goal and dream would work. But he kept at it and made his presence known there in Santa Monica. He regularly met with and engaged in conversation with these homeless guys—and it made a difference. They no longer felt that everyone looked past them and their needs. They no longer felt insignificant because there was at least one person who cared about them and what they were doing.

ALLOWING GOD TO CHALLENGE US

Although that experience didn't go so well for me, I did continue to move in this direction. I was challenged by my student's dream that God wanted to use us to meet the needs of people who are homeless. On a trip to San Francisco a few years later, I was sitting on a bus and really felt God saying I should talk to the guy next to me. But I didn't—and after I got off the bus I kicked myself because I had failed to do something that I really felt God wanted me to do.

Well, God wasn't going to let me off the hook because the next day in a totally different part of the city, I saw the same guy. This time I followed him (I know that sounds creepy) until he went into a record shop, and then I struck up a conversation about music. It didn't really go anywhere, but we at least talked for a solid hour and I felt like I was doing what God wanted.

Where the story gets a little weird—only God could come up with this kind of stuff—is that I ran into the same guy on the streets of Seattle the next summer! We quickly started talking again. He remembered me as the creepy record store guy, but we exchanged phone numbers saying we'd stay in touch.

God was up to something there. His dreams for me were bigger than my own. Had it been up to me, I probably would have quit being interested in caring about people who were homeless the minute that large soda was dumped on my head.

Kids and teenagers need to see us following dreams that come from God and believing that God has bold expectations for us. They need us to model what it means to take big steps and do things that seem countercultural or radical—all because God is leading. If we can give them the understanding that God is about bold expectations and dreams, it will make a huge difference in their faith journey.

THINK ABOUT:

1. When have you followed bold dreams and expectations? What results or experiences flowed from those actions?

2. How have you fostered that boldness in your own children—or in other young people within your sphere of influence?

3. When have you failed to believe that God could do something bigger than your dreams? What does it feel like to admit that? What can you learn from this?

PART 3:
MAKING CHANGES TO HELP OUR KIDS HAVE BOLD FAITH

It can feel overwhelming to think about the many changes and steps necessary to pass along a bold faith to your children. That's why this final section is filled with specific, practical tips and ideas that can help. Some of these are ideas I've already used in our family. Some of them reflect my years of church ministry. And others are new-to-me tips that I'll be trying out right along with you.

My advice is to pick one or two areas. Focus on these ideas, work through a few of them, and see what sticks. You may find that a particular thing really clicks with you and your faith journey. Do more of it. Similarly, something might not work for you at all. That's OK. We're all wired differently, so not everything will work well for every individual and every family. In other words, don't view it as a failure. For example, one area where I really struggle is reading my Bible in the morning. I wake up ready for my day and can't seem to focus right away on my Bible as my "first thing." I've had to learn to let that be OK. I finally figured out that after about two hours of work each morning, I'm ready to take a break, slow down, and spend time with the Lord through Scripture.

But I would also encourage you to keep trying some ideas just to see if you can reach a place where they work well for you. There may be times when you don't fully understand why something is important. Try it out a bit longer. Certain steps and practices may take a lot of work, but when you start seeing results in the faith lives of your children, you will be glad you put in the work.

The reality is that we as parents are the most important people in our children's faith journey, and how we live out our own faith really matters. In order to pass on a bold faith that helps our kids become more than just rule-keepers, we will need help from other people—family, friends, and other followers of Christ. I've written this section (this whole book, really) based on an assumption that you and your family are a part of a church. If you are not, you need to be because none of this can be done alone.

CHAPTER 13

ALLOWING QUESTIONS AND DOUBTS

I've been a longtime youth pastor and also a parent for nearly 13 years. I can say without a doubt that I'm way better at giving space for questions and doubts at youth group than I am at home. I guess it's just easier with someone else's kids than my own. With my own children, I really like it when they know what they believe—and ambiguity is scary. But we need to provide all kinds of opportunities for our kids to ask questions.

As I mentioned a few chapters back, one of my own children loves to ask questions. He's about to start fifth grade, and I still feel like I have a pretty good handle on answers for him. But every once in a while he'll ask me something that I don't fully know how to answer, so I'll have to dig deep to my Bible college and seminary roots and resources to come up with a suitable answer.

PREPARING FOR WHAT KIDS WILL ASK AND SAY

I can handle the questions now, but I'm worried about the first time one of my kids expresses doubt about their faith. That's going to be harder for me because my natural instinct will be to eradicate their doubt quickly by giving them all the reasons their doubt is not reasonable. I'll have to fight against that, though, because I know that's a horrible way to interact with anyone having doubt.

Sometimes we have to just sit with our doubt and let it be. I say this to college students all the time—that there will likely be points in their faith journey when they doubt, and at those moments they can stand on the foundation of their church and family and let them be the certainty for them. With my own kids, I have to be OK with their doubt and allow my faith and the way I live it out to be enough certainty of faith for them while they are experiencing the questions.

Here are a few tips that I think are important in understanding questions and doubts from young people.

Don't feel like you need to answer everything. It's really important that you don't feel you have to be the one to answer all of their questions. It's easy to answer questions that are basic about the Bible, but as kids get older and start asking deeper theological questions, you may just have to be OK sometimes with saying that you don't know. One thing I love about being Presbyterian and Reformed is that I can often rely on the answer that says, "I don't know, but because God is sovereign and in charge of all things, I just believe that he is right and doing it the way he wants." That may not satisfy every child, but we have to be OK sometimes with not answering every question. Perhaps the answer to a question needs to get "worked out" in the life of the child or student. Maybe the answer will come when they are on a mission trip, youth group event, talking to a relative, in the middle of a church service, or just spending time with other adults or friends. God reveals the right answer at the right time.

Provide different ways of expressing things. There are so many ways of expressing faith journeys and stories. In Western Christianity we are often overly enamored with words (pastors like me sure are), so we have to move beyond that and recognize that sometimes the way that our children need to figure out answers is different from how we found answers at their age. What if it's during a worship song, church service, story time, or through an art project? Recently in Costa Rica we asked children to draw out their view of God on some art paper. That was an incredible, eye-opening experience—seeing into the hearts and minds of young children as they shared with us what God looked like. So with your own kids, provide different ways of helping them express their faith.

Give them access to other people they can ask. This will come up multiple times in this section of the book, and I'll essentially say the same thing each time: You need help. Your children need to interact with other Christian adults who are modeling faith to them. Put other trusted adults in your children's lives and let them help you answer questions. They may have a totally different perspective from you that will really challenge your children to grow.

Be patient (even when it's hard). This is the toughest thing for me, and I even feel guilty writing about it. But I'm pointing the finger directly at myself and saying, "Listen up and learn!" We must be patient with our children and let them figure out what they think and believe. It might be their eighth question of the night that really gets to the heart of what they are struggling with. You may need to go through those first seven questions just so they trust you and your patience before they ask the zinger.

Ask your own questions, and share your own doubts. This may seem counterintuitive because asking questions feels like it could breed doubt in our own children. But we need to model the search for answers. When I don't know something or I'm feeling some doubt about where God is leading me, my family, or my ministry, it's so much better to say "I don't know" and then let my children see me praying and looking for answers than if I held it and just started moving in a direction I was unsure of. I realize this is probably easier as your kids get a little bit older, but I think it's important to model this in age-appropriate ways throughout our children's faith journey.

Talk to Sunday school teachers and ministry leaders about the need for questions and doubts. As a pastor who works with younger-age children and teenagers, I can't tell you how much I struggle when teachers shut down questions from students. And it makes me sad that a running joke in most Sunday school classrooms is that if students would just simply answer "Jesus" to any questions, they are likely to be right. We need to model healthy questions and answers in our Sunday school and vacation Bible school classrooms. We need children and teenagers to have the freedom to ask questions and not always get answers. As parents, we can step in and teach or talk to the teachers and help them know questions are OK.

Teach in a way that affirms questions. When you are teaching your own kids or sharing things with them, do it in a way that makes questions a common part of the interaction. If our children recognize that their questions matter in the little things, then when they start talking about and dealing with the big things, they will be so much better at asking questions.

THINK ABOUT:

1. What are some steps you can take to help your children ask more questions?

2. What steps can you take to be more open to questions and doubts?

3. How do you think you'd respond if one of your kids came to you today and said they don't believe in God?

4. What unresolved doubts or questions do you have about God or faith?

CHAPTER 14
FINDING JESUS-LOVING ROLE MODELS

Kids need to have friendships with older adults—not just their own parents—who love Jesus. Chap Clark and Kara Powell write about this in *Sticky Faith*. They flip around the original small group of five students to every one adult and say each student really needs five adults in their lives.[4] The first time I heard this, I was overwhelmed thinking about how that could practically work out. But the more I talked with other people, the more I realized that in many cases there are already multiple adults in our children's lives.

OUR CHILDREN NEED MULTIPLE ROLE MODELS

Let's use my son Soren as an example. Soren is an active kid who has a lot going on. He's involved in church and sports and has quite a few friends. Soren has a youth pastor named Nate, who just started at our church, and he is excited to get to know him. Nate will have a major impact in Soren's life. Soren also plays in the worship band, and the worship leader is a guy named John, who will impact him in big ways. Just around the corner from us live some good friends. Ron is the dad, a solid Christian, and he spends a ton of time with Soren both as a soccer coach and as the dad of one of his best friends. Another youth leader is Laura. She's been involved in Soren's life the last year and impacts him in great ways.

This summer there were two interns, Elliott and Hunter, who spent a lot of time with Soren and influenced him as young adults who love Jesus.

Our children need to interact with other trusted Christian adults because it provides them the opportunity to watch and see how Jesus is important to these adults. We all know that our kids can get frustrated with us because as parents we have to do a lot of things—including discipline! But some of these other adults can just love and care for our kids while walking them further down this faith journey.

I can't be Soren's youth pastor. Nate and Laura will be able to teach him things at church and on camps, retreats, and mission trips that I can't. He needs that. John, Hunter, and Elliott will all impact him in different ways that are so important to his journey. To be around these young men who love Jesus is such a life-giving thing for Soren. And Ron is a dad who is very different from me, so Soren is able to receive teaching about Jesus from a different perspective. This is all healthy.

Here are a few tips that I think are important to getting more trusted Christian adults involved in the lives of our children.

Help your children interact with adults. Start by writing a list of five adults who could help positively influence your children. They might be relatives, coaches, teachers, friends, youth workers, or Sunday school teachers. You probably have at least a couple of these connections already in place. Talk to those adults about your own hopes and desires for your children's faith. Pray for those adults. Ask God to use them to challenge and grow your kids.

Help facilitate those key relationships. I'm a "connector"—it's one of my major gifts and I love to use it. In the case of my kids, I want to be better at connecting and facilitating relationships with Christian adults. As the facilitator it's my job to regularly check in and provide two-way communication about my kids. These adults might need some info about how my kids are doing at home, and I might need to affirm them for how they are impacting my children. As a facilitator, we parents don't have to be the ones controlling everything—we just have to be helping those relationships grow. So there will be times you are just driving your children around as they interact with these other adults. That's OK. Releasing control of our kids and allowing God to work through other adults in their lives is a key area for us as parents. Maybe your role is to simply reach out to the pastors, volunteers, coaches, teachers, and other adults and let them know that you are on the same team—people who are all caring about your children.

Create rite-of-passage experiences for your kids. My oldest is about to turn 13. We are putting together a rite of passage for him on his birthday. We'll bring together all the Christian adults in his life that are local and spend part of a day doing something with him. Each adult will have some time to speak some truth about how they see Soren. For those who aren't local, we are asking them to write out some thoughts for him that we will compile into a book. This is how we plan on transitioning Soren to his teenage years. You can create rites of passage for younger kids, too. Anytime you have a major milestone, you can build something around it—even such events as starting kindergarten, receiving a Bible from church, taking communion for the first time, getting a puppy, or moving to a big-kid bed. We didn't create celebrations around all of those moments, but you can. The key is getting trusted Christian adults—particularly the closest ones—into the journey of faith and passage with your kids.

Give your children opportunities to serve with other adults. Service is a tremendous avenue for growth, especially when surrounded by trusted, mature adults. I recently returned from a mission project where we moved dirt, poured sand, and laid bricks. It took us four days to build this huge patio. Over the course of those days I worked with 23 students. The work was hard, and we had to really move quickly on the last day to get it all done. Children and students need to serve. Sadly, many churches and ministries don't provide enough opportunities. But as our children interact with other adults through service, they will really see the heart of those adults emerge. As we worked on the patio, I was particularly focused on the end use and how it would bless the ministry we were helping. I had multiple conversations with the students about their role in expanding the ministry of the church. Putting your children with other adults serving together will help them grow. You could do simple things such as having a lemonade stand for missions, passing out bulletins, planting flowers in a neighborhood house, painting backdrops for Sunday school classrooms, baking cookies for church, working with younger children, being on a drama team, or acting as greeters. There are so many ways that your children can serve alongside other trusted adults—you probably already have a bunch of ideas that could work.

Invite the youth and children's workers over for dinner. Let your children see their leaders in different contexts. As the facilitator of relationships, be aware of how to help build them. Inviting the leaders over to your house to see you interact as a family will give them a bit more of a perspective of how you live—and it will help them know how to better reach and interact with your children. This will be a big deal as your kids see these adults in your family context. I remember a bunch of years ago when my daughter's preschool teacher came to our house simply to see her room. This paid off in huge ways because my daughter no longer felt she had a teacher who was uninterested in her life—her teacher had seen where she slept and played.

Ask how you can get involved. My role is unique because I'm the boss of the youth ministry team. So I get to go on camps and retreats and see adults interacting with my children. But you can offer to help in various ways. You could be a volunteer at anything the church is doing with your kids. In fact, the ministry leadership would love to have you involved! You could go to camps and retreats and be engaged with your own kids as well as find yourself being one of those five adults in another child's life. You could volunteer as an assistant coach (not my gift) or bring snacks or treats for halftime or after the games. You could volunteer in the classroom (my wife does this a ton) to help with reading, grading, sorting papers, or decorating. Teachers love it when you ask to help. There are so many ways that you can get involved—you just need to come up with your list.

THINK ABOUT:

1. What key adults are involved in the lives of your children?

2. How are you facilitating more relationships between trusted Christian adults and your children?

3. Who are some adults that you haven't yet brought into your kids' faith journey that you want to?

4. What are some rite-of-passage experiences you might want to do with your children?

CHAPTER 15

ENCOURAGING GIFTS AND PASSIONS

My senior pastor, Scott, recently told me he believes the best people to be involved in a healing prayer ministry were probably children. His assertion was that children are uniquely set up to pray for healing and to be OK if God chooses not to heal someone right now. We adults struggle with God when he doesn't choose to heal someone. Children just move on. We haven't created a healing ministry for children yet, but we need to.

AFFIRM WHAT YOU SEE AND BELIEVE

Children have gifts and talents that we all recognize. It's easy to see when a child has basic talents such as art, singing, and drama. We can see when they are gifted in being able to focus, in reading or writing, in memorizing Scripture, and even in teaching simple yet profound things.

Far too frequently, we in the church don't give them opportunities to use those talents. Our programs, classes, camps, and retreats often aren't set up in ways that encourage our children to use their gifts and talents. But even in the home, we parents don't always do a good job of this either.

I want to spur you toward action—to thinking about ways that you can encourage your children to use their gifts and talents, and to affirm them when they do.

Here are a few tips aimed at creating new experiences for children so they can explore their gifts.

Give them opportunities to try new things. We all fall into patterns, and it can be hard to break free of them. In our parenting we tend to grab things that work—and keep doing them. Unfortunately, that habit also tends to carry over into our faith. Things like going to a worship service, attending Sunday school, and participating in youth group are all good but can be hindrances to growth if we simply stop there. We need to look beyond those things and try more. What if as a family you served in a convalescent home once a month? You might see something totally different come out in your kids. Try writing letters and becoming pen pals with church-sponsored missionaries. What if you attended a different style of worship service with your kids or taught in their Sunday school class? What might you see in them (and they in you) if you were engaged in different areas of ministry? We will only see the full picture of the gifts and talents of our own kids when we are able to see them in a variety of settings where those gifts can emerge and grow.

Go with them and engage. If you engage with your children and try out new things, they will likely see new and great gifts and talents in you—a reflection of your bold faith. I love to interact with people who are homeless—at least, I love to do it when I'm on mission trips where it's expected. But in my regular day-to-day life, I sometimes lose sight of this thing that I'm actually pretty good at doing. I need my kids to see me engaging with people who are in need—and I need them to see the gifts that God has given me get used to serve him. You need to engage and participate—not stand to the side—and see how God might use you and grow bolder faith in your life.

Try new things yourself. This can be tough for adults because we are often so set in our ways. But we have to be on the constant lookout for new ways that God might want to use us and use our talents. It's always fun to see someone do something for the first time and find out that they are good at it and that God blesses the experience. I love when people who don't think God could use them in youth ministry discover that they can make a difference in teenagers' lives. As they serve, it becomes incredibly clear that they are so gifted in sharing their faith journey. You may be in a rut with your faith. Take a big step and try new things—and involve your children with you. You will find out new things about each other.

You may have to change your family values. Yeah, this one hurts a little. You may need to change some of the things you've done over and over again. A young family in my church decided they were going to go on a mission trip. That whole year leading up to it, they saved money by not eating out on Fridays. That was a big value change and it was really hard for them, but they remember it as the biggest and best sacrifice while they prepared to go on this mission trip. You may have to re-evaluate vacations, Christmas presents, and other activities if you truly want to follow God. None of those things are bad, but what if those particular values and priorities are hindering you from following God in the way he wants?

In situations that allow it, let your children lead and help decide what you should do. I suspect that we as parents don't give our children enough opportunities to lead. What would it look like if you gave your children the task of doing a family devotion one night? They might do it in a totally different way than you expected, but it could be really good. My youngest loves to do plays. I can imagine giving her a Bible story and asking her to plan a play that we could all be a part of and see how that might impact us as a family. On different trips and events, releasing control (one of my biggest struggles) to our kids could be a great thing. Ask your children what things they would want to do to serve God or how they would like to engage in their faith. They eventually will have to do this on their own anyway, so giving them opportunities now can really be a good step.

Take time to affirm your kids. One area where we as parents must excel is in affirming our children when they are using their gifts and talents—even when we don't fully understand how it is all working out. Young people need affirmation. They are often told no on a regular basis, so we have to go above and beyond on their faith journey to say yes. This is hard sometimes as parents because we are so used to limiting them and what they can do, but when it comes to faith the answer needs to be yes more than no.

THINK ABOUT:

1. What are some of the gifts and talents you see in your children now?

2. What new things do you want to try in your own life?

3. How might you need to modify activities based on the ages of your children?

CHAPTER 16

ABANDONING COMFORT ZONES

We often find ourselves in a comfort zone that we don't want to leave. It could be as simple as a schedule that brings peace, order, and harmony to our family. I will fully admit that I like schedules and that timing is important to me. But sometimes I give that schedule too much value and importance. I lose sight of God when I'm so focused on having things done in the particular order and timing that works for my life. I know I'm called outside my comfort zone, and although it's hard to do sometimes, I have to be faithful in obeying God. It's not always easy to take those difficult steps, but doing it will change our faith in distinct and positive ways.

LEARNING HOW TO RELY ON JESUS

It's OK to admit that we like our comfort zones and places that don't make us anxious. But I think sometimes anxiety can be good in developing our faith because it forces us to rely on God even more. Faith grows and becomes bolder when we are forced to trust God. This is why in youth ministry we often create retreats and mission trips that put students in places where God becomes more "real" to them.

In your own family journey, you can create similar opportunities that get you and your children outside of your comfort zone and help you trust God more. These don't have to be major things or huge steps—you just want to get moving and see what God can do.

Here are a few things you can do that might take your family out of its comfort zone and challenge you to grow a bolder faith.

Take bold steps. This can be exciting and not scary. But the reality is that it's hard—so don't take too many all at once. Sit down and come up with one bold, major step for your family to do in the next month. It doesn't need to be that huge, expensive mission trip to Bolivia. Just think about what "bold" means for your family based on the ages of kids and stage of life you are in. Involve your children in planning the steps—and then do it.

Go on a mission trip. Again, this doesn't have to be a big, expensive trip overseas. My church just organized a daylong service project—and maybe that kind of event would be the ideal mission trip for your family. Or maybe you could do something in an inner city or a rural area in your state. The goal here is just that you commit to doing something that takes preparation and time to pull off. It would be key if there were other Christian adults involved because then you'd be accomplishing several faith-focused goals for your kids at once.

Serve at a soup kitchen. Most cities have these, and organizers will often allow younger children to serve alongside parents. Have a good conversation with your children beforehand and explain how some people are in need—and how Jesus wants us to care about basic needs such as food and shelter.

Start a neighborhood family group. This is a big push for a lot of families at my church right now, but it can be really hard to get going. As I already discussed, putting other Christian adults in your children's lives is important, so this helps meet that need. It also forces you to get out of your schedule rut and be engaged with others. It will benefit your family, your marriage, your children, and your neighborhood. You don't have to commit to doing a lifelong group. What if you just tried it for a month—maybe a meal together with a couple of other families every Sunday night? It could be as simple as one family reading a short devotional and everyone having a time of prayer.

Give more money, time, and resources. Being sacrificial with our time, money, and resources is a key component in fostering bold spiritual growth and getting out of ruts. When we focus more on others and less on ourselves, we begin to see things through Jesus' eyes and have the ability to live from his desires. You can and should start small here, but talk as a family about how could you use the gifts and talents God has given you to serve.

Start sponsoring a child in another country. We have done this with some success and some failure over the years. There was a season we were pretty good at showing our children pictures and reading them notes we received from our sponsored child. But then our child changed and we lost focus on that. You will find that with many children, this is a great way to help them focus on the world outside of themselves. Check with such organizations as Compassion International (compassion.com) and World Vision (worldvision.org) about the process for sponsoring a child.

Do a prayer walk in your city. What would it look like if you went into your city as a family and just spent time praying for different areas? This can be a cool thing to engage your kids in as they pray in specific areas. What if they lead your family prayer at their school and at the park, while you take the lead at city hall and the mall? Whenever you pray, have each family member ask God to reveal what to pray about and what to say.

Visit a different faith service. We recently went to a bat mitzvah for a friend's daughter. It was very eye-opening for our children. The way the Jewish faith reveres the Torah and handles it so carefully gave us a lot of things to talk about. The Hebrew language and the length of the service were great things to discuss, too. It really showed our children the good things about our own church as we compared and contrasted what they liked.

THINK ABOUT:

1. What patterns and things in your faith do you feel stuck in right now?

2. What things stand in the way of you having a bold faith?

3. How can you remove those obstacles? What part can other people play in helping you remove them?

4. What's one thing you can try as a family to explore bold faith together?

CHAPTER 17
MODELING IT YOURSELF

I just got back from a run. During my run, I prayed the whole time that God would make my faith bigger because lately a few things in my life have felt overwhelming and I've been forgetting how big my God is. I'm not sure if you are like me, but I often need to take an honest appraisal of my faith and then make some changes so that I can feel and see it grow.

HAVING SOMETHING WORTH MODELING

Our own faith journey is probably the most important thing that needs to be worked out in order for us to pass on bold faith to our children. It's pretty simple to understand that we spend more time with our own kids than anyone else does and that our faith is something they see demonstrated in life almost every day. So if our faith is weak, they can see it—and that can shake their faith because they're building on a weak foundation. I can't stress enough how much your faith matters.

I invite you to be open and honest about your faith and to think about how you might need to grow. In my own life, I know right now that I need to pray more. Prayer is the thing that centers my focus on Jesus and reminds me that he is the rock I build on. When I lose sight of that and my prayer life gets weak, I begin to lose focus.

But it might be something different for you. One thing we do in children's and youth ministries is to place a lot of different opportunities in front of students to give them many different things to try. You can do the same thing. Try praying more. Open up your Bible more often. Consider serving. Spend time in nature thanking God. All these things (and others) will help you develop a deeper faith and give you something worth modeling.

Here are a few ideas that can help get you out of any rut you may be stuck in and deepen your faith as you model it to your children.

What is your prayer life like? Prayer is talking to God, and when we aren't doing it, then we are missing out on a vital piece to this relationship. Think of it this way: If you chose not to talk to your spouse or kids for a month, how would it affect those relationships? But prayer can be more than just talking. In prayer we are listening to see what God wants us to know. We are reminded of who God is when we put him in the place he deserves. We proclaim God's might and goodness, and that can make the stuff we are dealing with feel so much smaller. I invite you to find a schedule that works for you and enter into a time of prayer more regularly. One thing I do is to pray when I'm driving. No, I don't close my eyes! I just talk to God as I'm going places. I find that more often than not, I have a greater sense of God when I arrive. You might try writing out your prayers or reading through Scripture as your prayer.

How often do you serve? Over the years, I have seen service become something so big in the lives of young people and their faith. But we get busy as adults and can forget how important it is. Think about how you might need to start serving. It could be in the church teaching a class, helping with parking, working in the nursery, or serving on a set-up or teardown team. Or it could be through a ministry that serves beyond the four walls of the church building. It's amazing how much more we get out of "going to church" when we have an active role in "being" the church.

Are you telling others about Jesus? This is a big step for a lot of us. You might be very comfortable with your faith, or maybe it's been a long time since you talked with someone about Jesus. I've gone through times when I seemed like I couldn't shut up, but sadly, too, there are times when I struggle to know how best to tell someone about God—even someone who is important to me. Take the risk and start by telling someone safe who is already a follower of Christ—then ask God to give you the boldness to talk with people who haven't come to faith in Jesus yet.

Do you invite people to church? Over the years I've become more and more convinced that we often ask children and students to do things that we are uncomfortable doing. Today I was so encouraged at church by several adults who introduced me to friends they had invited. It's a big deal to share this part of your life, and it can be hard. Inviting someone to church generally means having friends who aren't followers of Christ or who don't attend a church. That's a good thing if you are transparent with them—and they know what you believe they are expecting to get asked.

How can you praise God more than you already do? In my run today, I listened to praise music and I was lifting God up even when my run was pulling me down. I think one area in our faith journey we sometimes neglect is how we lift up and honor God. Try listening to music at home, in the car, or with headphones—and take some time to praise God.

Where do you read your Bible? I'm convinced that my kids need to see me read my Bible. One thing I fail at is reading my Bible in places where they will see me. I generally read a lot at my office at work, but that doesn't help my kids out. I need to be way more focused on this. We often do devotionals in the morning before school, and during breakfast time I should be reading and modeling this for my children. Where can you read your Bible so your children can see you?

Do you belong to a small group? This last year I joined a group of dads in my neighborhood. It was hard because I only knew one of the guys. The group meets in the evening, and I was already fairly busy all week. But I decided to commit, and it has made a big difference. As a pastor I read my Bible a lot when preparing messages and doing research, but I need more time to just read something and talk about it with a group of guys. I don't lead the study and don't answer all the questions either. These guys are slowly becoming my friends, and as a middle-age dad that's a big deal because it's hard to find. I like that my kids see me in a group with their friends' dads. It shows them that this faith thing is real to us and that we want to be bold.

How often do you read things aimed at growing your faith? You're already taking a meaningful step by reading this book. Good job! But there are plenty of other books out there that also can help your faith grow deeper and bolder. Ask around and see what people are reading, and then jump in. You don't have to finish it overnight. Put it in places where you can read a few pages at a time.

THINK ABOUT:

1. What are some steps you believe you need to take to grow deeper and bolder in your faith?

2. Which question in this chapter made you most uncomfortable, and why?

3. How can you put yourself in the best place to grow? Be specific.

CHAPTER 18
SUCCEEDING AND FAILING

Our children need to hear what we think they are good at—their strengths, their abilities, and their areas of potential and excellence. It's important for us to speak this truth into their lives over and over again—and I've been focusing on this practice a lot lately. As we parent and raise our children, we are the most important voices they will hear, and our role is so important.

HELPING KIDS LEARN FROM HIGHS AND LOWS

Affirmation is more than just saying "good job." It means showing that we fully understand what our kids are doing and that we are giving them positive encouragement for their gifts. I think back to a guy in my youth group years ago who showed some leadership talent. I began to speak into his life regularly and give him positive feedback about how he was using that leadership gift. I'm sure it wasn't just because of my affirmation, but he has become an incredible leader and is training to become a firefighter/paramedic.

It's easy to be negative and not affirm our children—or the young people in our sphere of influence. We as parents get busy, tired, and short in how we interact with them. We don't take the opportunity to praise enough, and we get caught in the trap of just pointing out when they do something wrong. This is a cycle that we must break because it doesn't raise bold children.

It does exactly the opposite—it can instill fear in our kids and make them afraid to try new things because they don't want to fail.

As we provide opportunities to succeed and fail, we have to walk alongside our children and let them know that we love them no matter what the results are. I have two sons who are very different. One is all about trying new things and is generally really successful at what he does. The other is more cautious and doesn't enjoy getting outside his comfort zone. The way I parent and provide opportunities to succeed and fail has to be different for each boy. Even the way I affirm is different. One son is all about high fives and "good jobs," while the other son would just rather I sit on the couch and talk with him.

Here are a few ideas that you can use to provide opportunities for affirmation, whether they succeed or fail.

How can you give them opportunities to safely fail? Try something hard. It should be just out of reach of what they can do, and walk through it with them as they try. What that thing should be will be different for every child. But remember that it's not just about the opportunity to try something risky and fail—it's also about coaching them through the entire experience and talking about how to best fail and how to learn from failures.

What kinds of affirmation do you give? It doesn't have to always be verbal. You could write a note, buy a milkshake, give a hug, sit and play a video game, read a book, pray at bedtime, or go on a walk. You'll have to figure out what kind of affirmation works for each child and then really work hard so that they hear you telling them, "Good job."

Set up activities where they can explore things going well or things going poorly. To be able to determine if something goes well or poorly, you need to set up the end results or metric against which you are judging. The easy thing to do here is to just make sure it is a pretty tough line and walk alongside your child as they try to achieve it. Or it could be something you don't set up—something that they are trying and you just spend time with them as it goes wrong. If it's something going well, offer truckloads of praise, and make sure your child knows he or she is doing a great job.

Pass out "Epic Fail" tickets, and really work to provide opportunities so they can use them. This might best work when your children are a little bit older, but encourage them to try things and give them a pass if it goes horribly wrong. My parents did this for me once when I was trying to make a milkshake and I fully destroyed the kitchen. It was so bad that I got chocolate sauce on the ceiling (no joke). But my mom just helped me clean it up, and I felt like I had learned something huge. If you use the tickets, be prepared for your children to redeem them at times you are not happy. You're going to have to really work on how you respond when something goes bad and a ticket gets flashed. At that point you are being watched.

THINK ABOUT:

1. What are some specific ways you've been successful in affirming your kids?

2. What are some specific things you could do that would affirm your kids for what they are already doing now?

3. What have you learned from failures in your own life? How can those lessons help you as a parent?

4. How might you need to respond when your son or daughter makes a major mistake?

CHAPTER 19

PARTNERING WITH OTHER PARENTS

One thing I've seen modeled in my life is how my wife's parents were deeply connected with other parents who really loved and cared for each other's kids. I joke that when I asked for my wife's hand in marriage I really had to ask five dads! Scary thought, right? It was sort of like that—but it's a powerful testimony to the strong friendships her parents had built.

SHARE THE JOURNEY WITH OTHER FAMILIES

If we believe that other Christian adults are a big deal in the lives of our children, then we as parents need to foster relationships with other families, too. Maybe you are a part of a church and are already surrounded by some families that are growing together. Or maybe you have a large extended family that is meeting this need. It could be that your sons or daughters have belonged to the same sports teams or organizations for a long time and you've really clicked with some of the other families.

Partnering with other parents isn't always easy. It's two or more completely different families coming together, and that can be messy and complicated. We lived next door to some dear friends for three years, and our kids really lived back and forth between both houses. It goes really well when everything clicks, but there are always going to be awkward parts. Those moments come with the territory, and if you are expanding your family to involve others, that will happen, too. But the payoff is huge as your kids get more opportunities to be with other adults and see how other families work. Plus your kids have all these other adults speaking into their lives. That's a win-win.

Here are some ideas of how you can partner with other parents.

Rites of passage with other families. I mentioned earlier that I value rites of passage. What if you invited other families to be a part of those rites? For example, what if getting a Bible from church in third grade was a really big deal and there were several other families who were involved in the lives of your children who came to a special service that was all about presenting that Bible? What if those other parents took the Bible and underlined verses and talked about what meaning those Scriptures had for them? Or you could do something where all the dads took a son away right as he was turning 13 to speak truth into his life about who he was and what they saw in him. There are so many things you could do, and involving other families is a huge win.

Small group/covenant group. As I alluded to a moment ago, my wife's parents' covenant group was a huge part of her life growing up. Those parents met monthly to synchronize calendars about what events they should be at in every one of the 15+ children's lives. This was a big deal, and my wife has really strong memories of all these families supporting her as she grew up. You can find and create this kind of group. Look at your church or just find other likeminded families in your neighborhood, schools, or extracurricular networks.

Vacations or events with other families. This category could include any activity you can think of aimed at building relationships and creating memories. As you pick families to be more intentionally engaged with, you will need to be equally intentional at doing things to get to know each other more. Those activities, events, and relationships should be aimed at helping everyone get to know each other's children and see what makes them tick.

Coaching, carpools, sleepovers, and campouts. There are so many things you could do to partner with other parents. Writing out a list here would be tough because the list would go on and on and on! Instead, I just want to encourage you to start writing a list.

THINK ABOUT:

1. What parents do you want to partner with more? Why?

2. What specific activities could you see yourself doing with other families?

3. What kind of small group do you have now? If you don't have one, do you want one? If so, how can you make it happen—and if not, why not?

CONCLUSION

I hope this simple book has provided you with specific, practical ideas for building a bolder faith in your own life and passing on a bold faith to your children—and to any other young people within your sphere of influence. This is an ongoing, never-ending adventure—you could go back and come up with a million other ideas to try, and you might still feel like you are struggling to pass on faith to your kids.

Fortunately, we're not in this alone. You and I are called to live a bold faith and to believe that with Jesus all things are possible. It is my hope that as we take steps in the right direction, our faith will grow and change our families, friendships, parenting, and how we interact with the world. When we become bold in our approach to our faith, it will change how we live.

Ultimately, we want to be bold parents who are raising our kids to be more than just rule-keepers. To do that, you will need to come up with your own plan that works for your family and your children. It'll take work because kids are different and have specific ways of working this out for themselves. My prayer is that as you ponder, discuss, and follow some of the ideas in this book, you will be traveling on the right path to figuring this out.

APPENDIX: BOOKS FOR PARENTS

Chap Clark. *Hurt 2.0: Inside the World of Today's Teenagers.* Grand Rapids, MI: Baker Academic, 2011.

Chap Clark and Dee Clark. *Daughters and Dads: Building a Lasting Relationship.* Colorado Springs, CO: NavPress, 1998.

Kenda Creasy Dean. *Almost Christian: What the Faith of Our Teenagers Is Telling the American Church.* New York, NY: Oxford University Press, 2010.

Robert C. Dykstra, Allan Hugh Cole Jr., and Donald Capps. *Losers, Loners, and Rebels: The Spiritual Struggles of Boys.* Louisville, KY: Westminster John Knox Press, 2007.

Robert Epstein. *Teen 2.0: Saving Our Children and Families From the Torment of Adolescence.* Fresno, CA: Quill Driver, 2010.

Steve Gerali. *Teenage Guys: Exploring Issues Adolescent Guys Face and Strategies to Help Them.* Grand Rapids, MI: Zondervan/Youth Specialties, 2006.

Mark Matlock. *Raising Wise Children: Handing Down the Story of Wisdom.* Grand Rapids, MI: Zondervan/Youth Specialties, 2012.

Mark Oestreicher. *Understanding Your Young Teen: Practical Wisdom for Parents.* Grand Rapids, MI: Zondervan, 2011.

Mark Oestreicher. *A Parent's Guide to Understanding Teenage Brains: Why They Act the Way They Do.* Loveland, CO: Group, 2012.

Mark Oestreicher and Adam McLane. *A Parent's Guide to Understanding Social Media: Helping Your Teenager Navigate Life Online*. Loveland, CO: Group, 2012.

Mark Oestreicher and Brooklyn Lindsey. *A Parent's Guide to Understanding Teenage Girls: Remembering Who She Was, Celebrating Who She's Becoming*. Loveland, CO: Group, 2012.

Mark Oestreicher and Brock Morgan. *A Parent's Guide to Understanding Teenage Guys: Remembering Who He Was, Celebrating Who He's Becoming*. Loveland, CO: Group, 2012.

Ginny Olson. *Teenage Girls: Exploring Issues Adolescent Girls Face and Strategies to Help Them*. Grand Rapids, MI: Zondervan/Youth Specialties, 2006.

John Palfrey and Urs Gasser. *Born Digital: Understanding the First Generation of Digital Natives*. New York, NY: Basic Books, 2008.

Kara Powell and Chap Clark. *Sticky Faith: Everyday Ideas to Build Lasting Faith in Your Kids*. Grand Rapids, MI: Zondervan, 2011.

Thom S. Rainer and Jess W. Rainer. *The Millennials: Connecting to America's Largest Generation*. Nashville, TN: B&H Publishing, 2011.

Christian Smith and Melinda Lundquist Denton. *Soul Searching: The Religious and Spiritual Lives of American Teenagers*. New York, NY: Oxford University Press, 2005.

Andrew Root. *The Children of Divorce: The Loss of Family as the Loss of Being*. Grand Rapids, MI: Baker Academic, 2010.

ENDNOTES

1. Dallas Willard, *The Divine Conspiracy: Rediscovering Our Hidden Life in God* (San Francisco, CA: Harper Collins, 1998), 41.

2. C.S. Lewis, *The Lion, the Witch and the Wardrobe* (New York, NY: Macmillan Publishing Co., 1970), 76.

3. Kenda Creasy Dean, *Almost Christian: What the Faith of Our Teenagers Is Telling the American Church* (New York, NY: Oxford University, 2010), 112.

4. Chap Clark and Kara Powell, *Sticky Faith: Everyday Ideas to Build Lasting Faith in Your Kids* (Grand Rapids, MI: Zondervan, 2011), 101.